The word "Pelican" and the depiction of a pelican are trademarks of Pelican Publishing Company, Inc., and are registered in the U.S. Patent and Trademark Office.

ISBN 9781455624614
Ebook ISBN 9781455624621

Printed in Malaysia

Published by Pelican Publishing Company, Inc.
1000 Burmaster Street, Gretna, Louisiana 70053
www.pelicanpub.com

To.......................................

From......................................

To my husband, Rob, for picking up the slack at home while
I pursued my dream! And to my original three dreams that
came true—Kyle, Sean, and Jaydi. Being your mom is the
icing on the gluten-free cake!—B. B. S.

To Katie, for being a determined comma!—M. A.

Katie squiggled around the chair legs. She swayed across the floor and wiggled up the side of a shelf. The shuffling footsteps of children coming near echoed in Katie's ears. The clever comma dove into a book to hide and landed at the end of a sentence.

Flo

POLAR BEARS

Katie gloomily left the book.

I'm Katie Comma.
I feel so alone.
I must keep searching
to find my way home.

Katie slithered under a chair.
She inched her way up the
leg to reach the top. She
traced around the edge of
the desk. Happy laughter
floated in from the hall. A
shadow passed by the door.
Katie quickly flipped into the
nearest book and landed at
the end of a sentence.

What is the

sum of

5

sorry!

Katie unhappily left the book.

I'm Katie Comma.
I feel so alone.
I must keep searching
to find my way home.

Katie squirmed over a carpet. She wove between the beanbags and curled up on a puffy pillow. Loud voices drifted closer to the classroom. Katie nervously shimmied inside the nearest book and twisted into the end of a sentence.

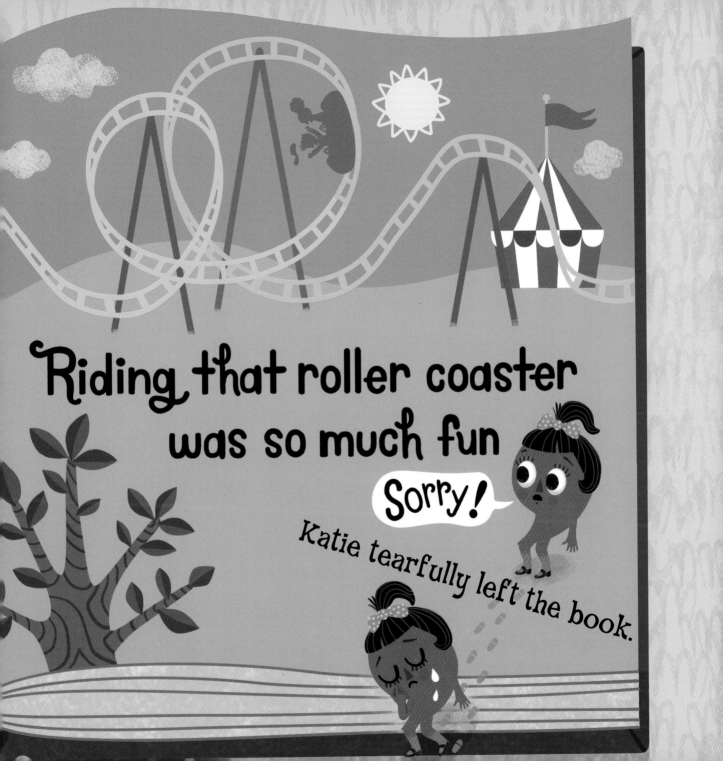

I'm Katie Comma.
I feel so alone.
Why keep on searching?
I don't have a home.

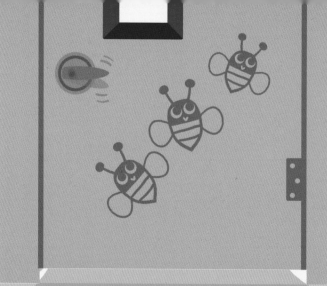

Katie wandered toward the classroom door. She climbed onto the teacher's desk and wobbled her way across the smooth surface. She heard the piercing ring of a bell. The doorknob jiggled. Katie plunged inside the nearest book and tumbled into the middle of a sentence.

The comma belongs in lists, in dates, in long numbers and before quotation marks.

The comma lists in dates and before

belongs in
in long numbers
quotation marks.

Katie couldn't believe her eyes! She stopped crying and gazed around the sentence. Katie stared into the faces of her family and knew she had found the place where she belonged.

I'm Katie Comma, and I'm not alone. I'm joyful, so lucky, and finally home!

Author's Note

I hope you enjoyed meeting Katie. As her Punctuation Pals would agree, commas are important, and we couldn't have stories without them. They are what make the difference between "Let's paint Mommy!" and "Let's paint, Mommy!"

But Katie is more than a curvy mark on the page. She's like you, someone trying to find her place in the world. Her story is about following your dreams, no matter what gets in your way. Some days are easy, but others make you feel as if those dreams will always be out of reach. Be like Katie and keep on trying, because one thing is for certain—your place is out there . . . waiting. Now, go find it.

Read and write on, my friends!